LPI Linux Essentials 010-160 Questions & Dumps

Exam Prep Questions for LPI 010-160 latest version

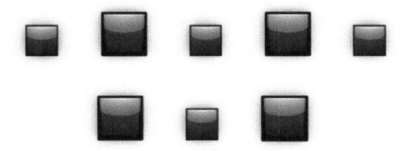

Authored By: Maxim Books

MAXIM BOOKS

About Maxim Books:

Maxim Books is a book publishing company incorporated in Dallas, Texas, USA, a place that is accessible both on the web and locally, which releases the force of education substances, Certifications guidebooks, poetry, and numerous other book genres. We make it simple for authors and writers to get their books planned, distributed, marketed, and sell expertly on an international scale with digital book + Print conveyance. Maxim Books was established in 2018 and expanding its business in more countries

Note: Answers of the questions are at the end of the book

QUESTION 1
What are the differences between hard disk drives and solid state disks? (Choose two.)

A. Hard disks have a motor and moving parts, solid state disks do not.
B. Hard disks can fail due to physical damage, while solid state disks cannot fail.
C. Solid state disks can store many times as much data as hard disk drives.
D. /dev/sda is a hard disk device while /dev/ssda is a solid state disk.
E. Solid state disks provide faster access to stored data than hard disks.

QUESTION 2
Reverse DNS assigns hostnames to IP addresses. How is the name of the IP address 198.51.100.165 stored on a DNS server?

A. In the A record for 165.100.51.198.ipv4.arpa.
B. In the PTR record for 165.100.51.198.in-addr.arpa.
C. In the RNAME record for 198-51-100-165.rev.arpa.
D. In the ARPA record for 165.100.51.198.rev.
E. In the REV record for arpa.in-addr.198.51.100.165.

QUESTION 3
What information can be displayed by top?

A. Existing files, ordered by their size.
B. Running processes, ordered by CPU or RAM consumption.
C. User accounts, ordered by the number of logins.
D. User groups, ordered by the number of members.
E. User accounts, ordered by the number of files.

QUESTION 4

Which of the following commands can be used to resolve a DNS name to an IP address?

A. dnsname

B. dns

C. query

D. host

E. iplookup

QUESTION 5

Which of the following outputs comes from the command free?

A.
```
A. 21:04:15 up 14 days, 7:43, 3 users, load average: 0.89, 1.00, 0.99
```

B.
```
avg-cpu:  %user    %nice    %system   %iowait  %steal  %idle
          34.04    0.03     13.88     1.06     0.00    50.99
```

C.
```
Filesystem             Size   Used   Avail   Use%   Mounted
                                                    on

/dev/mapper/vg_ssd-    25G    20G    3.6G    85%    /
root
```

D.
```
1.8M     /tmp
```

E.
```
        total      used      free     shared   buff/cache  available
Mem:  16123128  12565680  2011624   412128     1545824     7180416
```

QUESTION 6
What is the UID of the user root?

A. 1
B. -1
C. 255
D. 65536
E. 0

QUESTION 7
What is true about the owner of a file?

A. Each file is owned by exactly one user and one group.
B. The owner of a file always has full permissions when accessing the file.
C. The user owning a file must be a member of the file's group.
D. When a user is deleted, all files owned by the user disappear.
E. The owner of a file cannot be changed once it is assigned to an owner.

QUESTION 8
What information is stored in /etc/passwd? (Choose three.)

A. The user's storage space limit
B. The numerical user ID
C. The username
D. The encrypted password
E. The user\s default shell

QUESTION 9
Which of the following taroptions handle compression?
(Choose two.)

A. -bz
B. -z
C. -g
D. -j
-z2

QUESTION 10
Which of the following keys can be pressed to exit less?

A. l
B. x
C. e
D. q
E. !

QUESTION 11
Which of the following commands sorts the output of the command export-logs?

A. export-logs < sort
B. export-logs > sort
C. export-logs & sort
D. export-logs | sort
E. export-logs <> sort

QUESTION 12
A directory contains the following files:

```
a.txt

b.txt

c.cav
```

What would be the output of the following shell script? for file in *.txt
```
  do

    echo $file

  done
```

A. *.txt
B. a b
C. c.cav
D. a.txt
E. a. txt
   b. txt

QUESTION 13
Which of the following commands will search for the file foo.txtunder the directory /home?

A. search /home –file foo.txt
B. search /home foo. txt
C. find /home – file foo.txt
D. find /home –name foo.txt
E. find /home foo.txt

QUESTION 14
The current directory contains the following file:

-rw-r—r— 1 root exec 24551 Apr 2 12:36 test.sh

The file contains a valid shell script, but executing this file using ./test.shleads to this error:

bash: ./test.sh: Permission denied

What should be done in order to successfully execute the script?

A. The file's extension should be changed from .shto .bin.
B. The execute bit should be set in the file's permissions.
C. The user executing the script should be added to the execgroup.
D. The SetUID bit should be set in the file's permissions
E. The script should be run using #!./test. shinstead of ./test.sh.

QUESTION 15
What is a Linux distribution?

A. The Linux file system as seen from the root account after mounting all file systems.
B. A bundling of the Linux kernel, system utilities and other software.
C. The set of rules which governs the distribution of Linux kernel source code.
D. An operating system based on Linux but incompatible to the regular Linux kernel.
E. A set of changes to Linux which enable Linux to run on another processor architecture.

QUESTION 16
Which package management tool is used in Red Hat-based Linux Systems?

A. portage
B. rpm
C. apt-get
D. dpkg
E. packagectl

QUESTION 17
Why are web browser cookies considered dangerous?

A. Cookies support identification and tracking of users.
B. Cookies are always public and accessible to anyone on the internet.
C. Cookies consume significant amounts of storage and can exhaust disk space.
D. Cookies store critical data which is lost when a cookie is deleted.
E. Cookies can contain and execute viruses and malware.

QUESTION 18
Which of the following are typical services offered by public cloud providers? (Choose three.)

A. Platform as a Service(PaaS)
B. Infrastructure as a Service(IaaS)
C. Internet as a Service(IaaS)
D. Graphics as a Service (GaaS)
E. Software as a Service (SaaS)

QUESTION 19
Which of the following characters in a shell prompt indicates the shell is running with root privileges?

A. !
B. #
C. *
D. &
E. $

QUESTION 20
What is true about a recursive directory listing?

A. It includes the content of sub-directories.
B. It includes the permissions of the directory listed.
C. It includes details of file system internals, such as inodes.
D. It includes ownership information for the files.
E. It includes a preview of content for each file in the directory.

QUESTION 21
Which of the following directories contains information, documentation and example configuration files for installed software packages?

A. /usr/share/doc/
B. /etc/defaults/
C. /var/info/
D. /doc/
E. /usr/examples/

QUESTION 22
Which of the following commands adds the directory /new/dir/ to the PATHenvironment variable?

A. $PATH=/new/dir: $PATH
B. PATH=/new/dir: PATH
C. export PATH=/new/dir: PATH
D. export $PATH=/new/dir: $PATH
E. export PATH=/new/dir: $PATH

QUESTION 23
A user is currently in the directory /home/user/Downloads/ and runs the command

Is ../Documents/

Assuming it exists, which directory's content is displayed?

A. /home/user/Documents/
B. /home/user/Documents/Downloads/
C. /home/user/Downloads/Documents/
D. /Documents/
E. /home/Documents

QUESTION 24
Which of the following is a protocol used for automatic IP address configuration?

A. NFS
B. LDAP
C. SMTP
D. DNS
E. DHCP

QUESTION 25
Which of the following devices represents a hard disk partition?

A. /dev/ttyS0
B. /dev/sata0
C. /dev/part0
D. /dev/sda2
E. /dev/sda/p2

QUESTION 26
What can be found in the /proc/directory?

A. One directory per installed program.
B. One device file per hardware device.
C. One file per existing user account.
D. One directory per running process.
E. One log file per running service.

QUESTION 27
A new server needs to be installed to host services for a period of several years. Throughout this time, the server should receive important security updates from its Linux distribution.

Which of the following Linux distributions meet these requirements? (Choose two.)

A. Ubuntu Linux LTS
B. Fedora Linux
C. Debian GNU/Linux Unstable
D. Ubuntu Linux non-LTS
E. Red Hat Enterprise Linux

QUESTION 28
Which of the following directories must be mounted with read and write access if it resides on its own dedicated file system?

A. /opt

B. /lib

C. /etc

D. /var

E. /usr

QUESTION 29
The ownership of the file doku.odtshould be changed. The new owner is named tux. Which command accomplishes this change?

A. chmod u=tux doku.odt

B. newuser doku.odt tux

C. chown tux doku.odt

D. transfer tux: doku.odt

E. passwd doku.odt:tux

QUESTION 30
What happens to a file residing outside the home directory when the file owner's account is deleted? (Choose two.)

A. During a file system check, the file is moved to /lost +found.

B. The file is removed from the file system.

C. The UID of the former owner is shown when listing the file's details.

D. The user root is set as the new owner of the file.

E. Ownership and permissions of the file remain unchanged.

QUESTION 31
What is true about links in a Linux file system?

A. A symbolic link can only point to a file and not to a directory.
B. A hard link can only point to a directory and never to a file.
C. When the target of the symbolic link is moved, the link is automatically updated.
D. A symbolic link can point to a file on another file system.
E. Only the root user can create hard links.

QUESTION 32
Which files are the source of the information in the following output? (Choose two.)
uid=1000 (bob) gid=1000 (bob) groups=1000 (bob), 10 (wheel), 150 (wireshark), 989 (docker), 1001 (libvirt)

A. /etc/id
B. /etc/passwd
C. /etc/group
D. /home/index
E. /var/db/users

QUESTION 33
Which of the following tasks can the command passwd accomplish? (Choose two.)

A. Change a user's username.
B. Change a user's password.
C. Create a new user account.
D. Create a new user group.
E. Lock a user account.

QUESTION 34
Which command displays file names only and no additional information?

A. ls -a

B. ls -lh

C. ls -l

D. ls -alh

E. ls -nl

QUESTION 35
Which of the following commands puts the lines of the file data.csvinto alphabetical order?

A. a..z data.csv

B. sort data.csv

C. abc data.csv

D. wc -s data.csv

E. grep --sort data.csv

QUESTION 36
Which of the following examples shows the general structure of a forloop in a shell script?

A. for *.txt as file => echo $file

B. for *.txt (echo $i)

C. for file in *.txt do
        echo $i done

D. for ls *.txt exec {} \;

E. foreach @{file} { echo $i
    }

QUESTION 37
What is the return value of a shell script after successful execution?

A. 1

B. 0

C. -1

D. -255

E. 255

QUESTION 38
Which of the following statements are true regarding a typical shell script? (Choose two.)

A. It has the executable permission bit set.

B. It starts with the two character sequence #!.

C. It is located in /usr/local/scripts/.

D. It is located in /etc/bash/scripts/.

E. It is compiled into a binary file compatible with the current machine architecture.

QUESTION 39
Which of the following commands extracts the contents of the compressed archive file1.tar.gz?

A. tar -czf file1.tar.gz

B. ztar file1.tar.gz

C. tar -xzf file1.tar.gz

D. tar --extract file1.tar.gz

E. detar file1.tar.gz

QUESTION 40
Which of the following commands finds all lines in the file operating-systems.txtwhich contain the term linux, regardless of the case?

A. igrep linux operating-systems.txt
B. less -i linux operating-systems.txt
C. grep -i linux operating-systems.txt
D. cut linux operating-systems.txt
E. cut [Ll] [Ii] [Nn] [Uu] [Xx] operating-systems.txt

QUESTION 41
Which of the following programs are web servers? (Choose two.)

A. Apache HTTPD
B. Postfix
C. Curl
D. Dovecot
E. NGINX

QUESTION 42
Which of the following Linux Distributions is derived from Red Hat Enterprise Linux?

A. Raspbian
B. openSUSE
C. Debian
D. Ubuntu
E. CentOS

QUESTION 43
What are the differences between a private web browser
window and a regular web browser window? (Choose
three.)

A. Private web browser windows do not allow printing or
storing websites.
B. Private web browser windows do not store cookies
persistently.
C. Private web browser windows do not support logins into
websites.
D. Private web browser windows do not keep records in the
browser history.
E. Private web browser windows do not send regular stored
cookies.

QUESTION 44
What is the preferred source for the installation of new
applications in a Linux based operating system?

A. The vendor's version management system
B. A CD-ROM disk
C. The distribution's package repository
D. The vendor's website
E. A retail store

Answers

1. Correct Answer: AE

2. Correct Answer: B

3. Correct Answer: B

4. Correct Answer: D

5. Correct Answer: E

6. Correct Answer: E

7. Correct Answer: A

8. Correct Answer: BCE

9. Correct Answer: BD

10. Correct Answer: D

11. Correct Answer: D

12. Correct Answer: E

13. Correct Answer: D

14. Correct Answer: B

15. Correct Answer: B

16. Correct Answer: B

17. Correct Answer: A

18. Correct Answer: ABE

19. Correct Answer: B

20. Correct Answer: A

21. Correct Answer: A

22. Correct Answer: E

23. Correct Answer: D

24. Correct Answer: E

25. Correct Answer: D

26. Correct Answer: D

27. Correct Answer: AE

28. Correct Answer: D

29. Correct Answer: C

30. Correct Answer: CE

31. Correct Answer: D

32. Correct Answer: BC

33. Correct Answer: CE

34. Correct Answer: A

35. Correct Answer: B

36. Correct Answer: C

37. Correct Answer: B

38. Correct Answer: AE

39. Correct Answer: C

40. Correct Answer: C

41. Correct Answer: AE

42. Correct Answer: E

43. Correct Answer: BDE

44. Correct Answer: C

www.ingramcontent.com/pod-product-compliance
Lightning Source LLC
LaVergne TN
LVHW081808050326
832903LV00027B/2149